The *Very* Generic and Experiential
Zodic-Based Guide to
Valentines Day Bliss

by Beth McDonald & Jamie O'Toole
artwork by Jamie O'Toole

Copyright © 2013

First edition, 2008
Second edition, 2013

Dedication

This book is dedicated to
all those who have ever had the courage to love
and somehow managed to keep
a sense of humor about it.

The Very Generic and Experiential
Zodiac-Based Guide to Valentine's Day Bliss

Greetings and Happy Valentine's Day!

Welcome to the second edition of our first book. For those of you who may not know, I have done a *"Very Generic and Experiential Zodiac-Based Holiday Shopping Guide"* for years and it has been quite popular. Right off the bat people were asking for a Valentine's Day version, but I couldn't figure out the right way to go about it.

The biggest stumbling block for me was the Moon placement which, in Astrology, serves as the biggest determiner of how someone gives and receives love. Because of this, the Moon placement is more important than the Sun on matters of romance. As most people do not know their own Moon sign, much less the Moon sign of their partner – speaking to that initially seemed impossible to do accurately.

Also complicating matters was the reality that different couples often celebrate Valentine's Day very differently. Usually this is reflected by the placement of the Moon in their Composite chart. To make a very long story very short, for some couples Valentine's Day is the most romantic moment of their year. For others, it is just the tiniest of blips on their annual radar screen.

Lastly, is the gender factor. As much as we all try to pretend this isn't an issue, men and women generally have very different needs around and perceptions of Valentine's Day. A Taurus man will approach this holiday very differently than a Taurus woman. Hence, there is a high percentage of men who feel totally pressured to perform and women who feel disappointed. It's no wonder people were asking for a little help here.

 I was only too happy to oblige – if I could only find the way in. Finally, when I was editing the Holiday Shopping Guide in 2005, the solutions came to me. Actually, it and gift categories came to Eric (thanks, babe). He suggested I just make gift suggestions for the different Sun signs. That way everyone can work with what they know.

So here it is. This shopping guide has a very different format than the others, but it has been just as much fun to write. Perhaps more so. I hope it's as fun to use! For those of you who don't know your lover's Moon sign, this will be enough to get you where you are trying to go by referring to your lovers Sun sign. For those of you who actually do know your lover's Moon Sign, take that sign's information as listed in these pages and multiply it *exponentially*. Explore and experiment and let me know what you think, and how it works for you and yours. And may it contribute to many, many, many blissful Valentine's Days!

Xoxoxox
b

March 21 – April 20

Aries

Aries

Ruled by Mars, the God of War, Aries is probably the least romantic of all the signs. Also, as the archetype of Divine Male, Aries is more masculine, athletic, and physical and therefore not remotely interested in the mushy and the froufrou. Love is just not their strong suit – love is their *life lesson*, so you sort of have to show them the way. God help you if your lover is an Aries or has a lot of Aries in their natal charts, for the traditional, romantic sort of gifts are just not going to carry as much weight with them as they would for a *normal* person. The Valentine's Day experience you are trying to create for them doesn't need to say "*I love you*" as much as it needs to say "*You just rock.*"

Excursions & Adventures: The gym, base jumping, or heli-skiing.

Valentine's Day Meal: A picnic at a scenic outdoor location where you can enjoy the sunset, after partaking of some seriously athletic and strenuous activities like running, biking, beach volleyball, or hiking up the highest peak in town.

Songs for the iPod: The Beatles, "*Why Don't We Do It In The Road?*"
Frank Sinatra, "*I Did It My Way*"
Vitamin C, "*Me, Myself, and I*"

Books for the Library: For Him: "*Sports Illustrated Swimsuit Knockouts: 5 Decades of Swimsuit Photography*"
For Her: A GQ magazine subscription.

DVD: Anything by Warren Miller, preferably the collection.
"*Austin Powers: International Man of Mystery*"
"*Superman*"

Trinket: For Him: A hat with the logo of his beloved car on it.
For Her: A red candle, preferably scented with her favorite aroma.

Tickets to something: A sporting event, preferably a championship, like the Stanley Cup or the NBA playoffs. Car shows like the Barrett-Jackson or the Concourse d'Elegance car shows.

Clothing: Hats with the emblems of their favorite sports teams.

Foreplay: Massages.

Mantra to help you get on the right page:
Forgive them, Father, for they know not what they do.

APRIL 21 – MAY 20

Taurus

Taurus

Contrary to Aries, Taurus *rules* romance, beauty, harmony, and the divine feminine archetype. If your lover is a Taurus or has a lot of Taurus in their natal charts, Valentine's Day for you is the retailers' equivalent of Christmas – everything you do the whole rest of the year depends on what happens right here, right now. *Oh,* and how well you perform under intense pressure. Sorry, baby, but this is just not negotiable. You will need to really get this right, or there'll be a dog house out back with your name on it. The safe bet is to fall back on the normal traditions. All of them. Now is not the time to get experimental, cheap, or to cut corners. I am talking the *full monty* here. If you are not showing up with at least the traditional Valentine's Day Trifecta – jewelry, chocolate, and flowers – don't show up at all.

Excursions & Adventures: All your beloved's favorite retail outlets for jewelry, clothing, and, if you are loving a woman, shoes.

Valentine's Day Meal: Something quiet and intimate, expensive and tasteful. If you can't make up your mind, default to the best place in town.

Songs for the iPod: Joe Cocker, *"You are So Beautiful"*
Perry Como, *"It Had to Be You"*
James Blunt, *"Beautiful"*
Hole, *"Boys on the Radio,"* and *"Reasons to be Beautiful"*

Books for the Library: *"Queer Eye for the Straight Guy: The Fab 5's Guide to Looking Better, Cooking Better, Dressing Better, Behaving Better, and Living Better"*

DVD: *"Shrek"*
"Cleopatra"

Trinket: No trinkets. *Gifts.* There should be several and they should not be sale items. At least one of them better be jewelry (nothing less than a carat), and not the fake stuff.

Tickets to something: Fashion shows in New York, Paris, or Milan. Art shows, exhibits, or openings.

Clothing: A large necklace with gemstones for her, preferably diamonds. Some Armani neckwear for him.

Foreplay: A bath together in a tub full of rose petals and essential oil.

Mantra to help you get on the right page:
Love is all you need.

May 21 – June 20

Gemini

Gemini

The sign of Gemini is governed by Mercury, who was the messenger of the Gods. Because of this, Gemini is said to rule how you think, how you speak, and how you communicate. So if you are in love with anyone with the slightest bit of Gemini in their natal charts, it's all about the words, baby. Romance is nice, but your gifts and gestures will be better received if they are coupled with a little something verbal, as well. You need something that stimulates your lover *above* the neck. Your Valentine's Day gift needs to say, "*You are truly brilliant, and I love your warped and fragile little mind.*" Because they are so bloody mental, Geminis are notoriously complicated people, and loving them can be a daunting task. Certainly not for the timid. However, they are generally very mutable and even more distractible. This means if you love a Gemini, while it may be harder work, you have a greater margin for error.

Excursions & Adventures: No adventures, given your Gemini's tendencies towards getting distracted and then lost, in that order. It's just not wise.

Valentine's Day Meal: Must be eclectic: either a smorgasbord or some place where there are a lot of choices. A lot of very different choices.

Songs for the iPod: Louis Armstrong, "*Hello Dolly*"
Bobby Darin, "*Mack the Knife*"
Anything by 10,000 Maniacs

Books for the Library: "*10,000 Answers: The Ultimate Trivia Encyclopedia*"
"*The Harper Book of Quotations*"
"*The Complete Oxford English Dictionary*"
(all 13 volumes, bound)

DVD: "*Rain Man*"
"*A Beautiful Mind*"
The box set of "*Malcom in the Middle*"

Trinket: "*The 100 Best Love Poems of all Time*"

Tickets to something: Comedy clubs and shows, Leno, or a film festival. A trip to the Sunglass Hut (see following).

Clothing: Sunglasses.

Foreplay: Reading.
Dirty, nasty, absolutely obscene pillow talk (preferably whispered in their ear).

Mantra to help you get on the right page:
:
I am really interested in listening to what he/she is talking about.
I really care about listening to what he/she is talking about.
I really want to listen to what he/she is talking about.

June 21 - July 20

Cancer

Cancer

Cancer rules home and hearth, and most of those governed by the sign of Cancer don't like to stray too far from it. Ever. Under any circumstances. Cancerians identify themselves by the homes they live in and also by the families they belong to - often quite extended . If your lover is a Cancer or is someone who has a lot of Cancer in their natal chart, not only will they be unable to stop talking about their families, they cannot talk about anything else. You can't have a conversation with a Cancer without them bringing up their families, identifying every single one of them by name and age. A most annoying habit. For them, your Valentine's Day gift needs to say much more than *"I love you,"* it needs to say *"I love it that we are a family."* A word of caution here: Just like its namesake, the Crab, your Cancer lover can have a hard exoskeleton that is difficult to penetrate. So you may have to be diligent to get your message across. To make matters even more, um, *interesting,* Cancer is ruled by the Moon, which serves to make your Crab's moods ebb and flow just like it does the tide. Stay calm and clear and consistent and you'll be okay. And wear a life jacket.

Excursions & Adventures: A trip to Home Depot, followed by a sweep through Linens 'N' Things and then the Pottery Barn.

Valentine's Day Meal: Something special that you cook together at home, before snuggling on the couch and watching anything on the Food Network or HGTV on your home theatre system.

Songs for the iPod: Sonny & Cher, *"I Got You Babe"*
Sister Sledge, *"We Are Family"*
Wings, *"Mull of Kintyre"*
CSN&Y, *"Our House"*

Books for the Library: *"The Western Garden Book,"* or a subscription to *"Sunset Magazine," "Architectural Digest,"* or *"Better Homes and Garden"*

DVD: *"National Lampoon's Vacation"*
"Bringing Up Baby"
"The Brady Bunch"

Trinket: A tree or something to plant in the yard. Decorative stoneware. Bowls and vases.

Tickets to something: A home and garden show.

Clothing: Warm wooly sweaters for him; purses and shoes for her.

Foreplay: Cleaning out the attic or garage together. Looking through old photograph albums or watching home movies. Planning to visit relatives on your next vacation, or make a baby.

Mantra to help you get on the right page:
There's no place like home. There's no place like home. There's no place like home.

Leo

Leo

Leo is the sign of kings, so if your lover has significant Leo in their natal charts, their complete and total rulership of your heart and soul needs to be redundantly acknowledged. Your gift needs to say, "*You are worshipped and adored.*" Leo also rules the heart, so this is sort of their day. They absolutely love dramatic demonstrations, so nothing short of a Busby Berkeley-style production number will do. I'm talking a cast of *thousands*. If you feel like your Valentine's Day plans are a little over the top, you are probably right on track. Leo also rules risk-taking and gambling, so if you are pushing the edge of some envelope you will definitely score some bonus points. And don't forget fun. It has to be fun, because not fun is boring and bored kitties tear up your favorite things and then take naps. Nobody wants to see that. Lastly and probably most important for you, don't forget that Leo is, after all, the Lion: affectionate, generous, warm, and loving when happy, and will hunt you down, kill you, and eat you when displeased. Note to self: Don't f'&% this up!

Excursions & Adventures: Dinner and gambling at a casino.

Valentine's Day Meal: Some place neither of you have ever been before, preferably a place that looks like it might have failed a health department inspection or two. Or perhaps a dinner theater. Bonus points if both.

Songs for the iPod: The entire soundtrack from "*Cats*"
Harry Nilsson's "*Coconut*" (Actually, anything by Nilsson)
James Taylor's "*Shower the People*"
Mel Torme's "*Hello Young Lovers*"

Books for the Library: Doesn't matter, cats don't read.

DVD: Mutual of Omaha's "*Wild Kingdom*"
"*Born Free*"
"*Daktari*"
Anything on Animal Planet

Tickets to something: The Lottery.

Clothing: Leather pants and fur coats. (I know. Not politically correct, but cats don't care what you think.)

Foreplay: Lying around on the rug by the fire and preening.

Mantra to help you get on the right page:
Here, kitty, kitty, kitty …

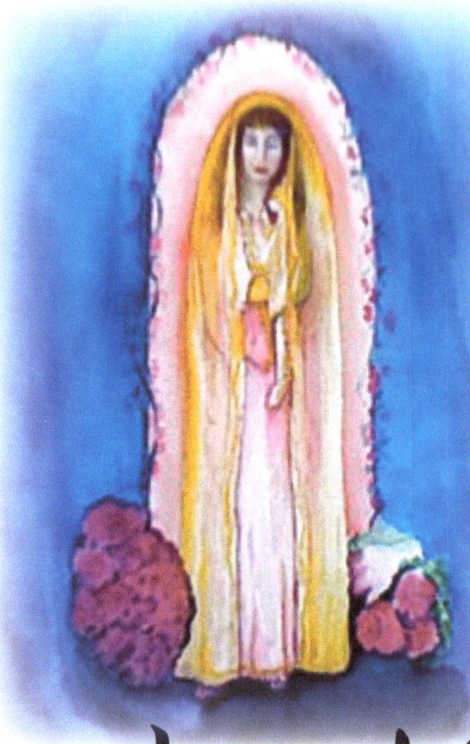

August 21 – September 20

Virgo

Virgo

Virgo is hard to love, for two reasons. The first is they are pretty damn particular. The second, and infinitely more noble, is anyone who incarnated as a Virgo primarily came here to be of service to others, therefore their modus operandi is more about giving than receiving, loving rather than being loved. Receiving is a life lesson for them. Actually, it's more than that – learning how to receive is the ultimate life lesson for them – and as such it is going to be the hardest thing for them to do. So on Valentine's Day and birthdays, when they have to stretch a bit (or a lot), these guys can sometimes be uncomfortable. Sometimes very uncomfortable. Sometimes even a bit peckish, so be patient. You will be better off if you go with subtle and understated, as they overwhelm easily. Virgo needs one or two small, simple, basic gifts: flowers, or jewelry, or a heart shaped box of chocolates (just not the big one). Your gift to them needs to say, *"Try to begin to think about believing that you are worthy."*

Excursions & Adventures: Don't even try, it's just not what they do and it will only upset them. Offer to just hang out and do something they like doing. Especially if it involves cleaning, fixing, or repairing something.

Valentine's Day Meal: Doesn't matter much, as long as the place is spotlessly clean, doesn't cost a lot of money, and they've been there before. Virgos do not like surprises. Though you will get bonus points for a health food place, especially if it is vegetarian.

Songs for the iPod: U2, *"Bad"*
The Kinks, *"The Alcohol Song"*
Johnny Cash, *"I Walk the Line"*
Pretenders, *"Back on the Chain Gang"*

Books for the Library: *"Emily Post's Etiquette"*

DVD: *"My Fair Lady"*
The complete box set of *"The Odd Couple"*

Trinket: A gift certificate for a couple of sessions each with a professional organizer and a feng shui practitioner.

Clothing: Several sets of Yoga clothes, preferably white, they can wear a couple of times and then give to the Goodwill so someone less fortunate can use them. Anything from the Victorian or Edwardian eras or made in that style.

Foreplay: A crossword puzzle, cleaning out the fridge together.

Mantra to help you get on the right page:
What would Jesus do?

SEPTEMBER 21 – OCTOBER 20

Libra

Libra

Librans are the peacemakers of the universe. As such, they are definitely lovers, not fighters. So you would think Valentine's Day would be one of the easier holidays for those who love them. Tragically, that's not the case. Just as the scales go back and forth before finding balance, so do Librans. These folks have always got some personal struggle for balance going on; their life lesson is to figure out how to make peace with their perfectly imperfect little world. So the ideal gift for them, the thing that would truly make them the happiest, is something that involves or engenders some sort of moral dilemma. At a bare minimum it should be a little less than perfect. To truly make your Libra happy, your gift should reflect the yin and yang of life, echo both the dark side and light side of the force, and have some sort of little flaw in it. Your gift needs to say, *"Wrangle on, baby."*

Excursions & Adventures: Art museums, architectural tours, and peace rallies. The Franklin and Eleanor Roosevelt Institute, or the University of Arkansas Clinton School of Public Service.

Valentine's Day Meal: Doesn't matter much, as long as the place and the food taste and look aesthetically pleasing, yet mediocre, and you both (sort of) like it. And if you want to score a home run, make sure it is also some place where you can pretty much guarantee there will be a long wait and the surly help will give you crappy service.

Songs for the iPod: Charlotte Church, *"There's a Place for Us"*
Helen Reddy, *"I Don't Know How To Love Him"*
The Clash, *"Should I Stay or Should I Go"*

Books for the Library: *"The Long Walk to Freedom,"* by Nelson Mandela
"The Crucible," by Arthur Miller
"Madame Secretary," by Madeleine Albright
Anything on the mediation process, the history of women's suffrage, or the history of the civil rights movement.

DVD: *"The Turning Point," "Casablanca," "The Red Shoes,"* or *"Anatomy of a Dancer." "Dr. Strangelove, or: How I Learned to Stop Worrying and Love the Bomb"*

Clothing: Factory seconds, anything from a thrift store, preferably that used to be owned by a Virgo (see Virgo).

Foreplay: A nice cup of hot herbal tea over a lengthy and lively intellectual discussion of how best to bring peace and equality to all of the earth's people by stopping global warming, ending hunger, and more evenly distributing the worlds' resources.

Mantra to help you get on the right page:
We shall overcome.

October 21 – November 20

Scorpio

Scorpio

This holiday is not a tough one for Scorpios. Aside from Beltane (the ancient spring fertility celebration), Valentine's Day is a Scorpio's best and most favorite holiday. Not so much because of the love thing but because the love thing gives them temporary, though utter and complete, permission to indulge one of their favorite passions: *passion*. Scorpio is the most passionate of all the signs, and Valentine's Day gives them complete license to unleash their passions, every single little one of them. Particularly, sex. Your Scorpio should be pretty easy to please if you focus on their absolute favorite pleasures and vices. If your lover is a Scorpio or has the slightest shred of Scorpio in their natal charts, your gift needs to say, *"Do Me."*

Excursions & Adventures: The adult bookstore.

Valentine's Day Meal: Each Other. Skip the meal and go straight to the hotel. You can order room service later.

Songs for the iPod: The Grateful Dead, *"Mama Tried"*
Janis Joplin, *"Summertime"*
Beck, *"Sexx Laws"*
George Michael, *"I Want Your Sex"*
Animotion, *"Obsession"*
Heart, *"Magic Man"*
Al Green, *"Let's Get it On"*
Anything by the Libertines

Books for the Library: *"The Kama Sutra"*
"The Tibetan Book of the Dead"
"How to Avoid Being Prosecuted for Tax Evasion for Dummies"
Anything by the Marquis De Sade.

Trinket: Calvin Klein's *"Obsession"*

DVD: Your own. Don't forget to bring the video camera.
"The Usual Suspects," "Mr. & Mrs. Smith," James Bond box set,
"Rat Race," "A Streetcar Named Desire,"
"Death Takes a Holiday," "Meet Joe Black"

Clothing: No clothes, they prefer being naked. But if you must, get lingerie or something tear-away that you both can take off very quickly. Or perhaps one of those lovely orange prison jumpsuits.

Foreplay: A trip to your attorney's or bail bondsman's office, or perhaps to their favorite tattoo parlor for some new ink or piercings.

Wild Card: Dress up like a law enforcement officer and handcuff yourself to something.

Mantra to help you get on the right page:
OH YES! YES! YES! YES!

November 21 – December 20

Sagittarius

Sagittarius

Unless there are majorly contrary indicators in their natal charts, Sagittarians are by far the easiest to love. Especially if you have too much earth in your chart. Ruled by Jupiter, the God of Luck, Sagittarians just want everyone to be happy, to have fun, and let the good times roll. Life and love seems to flow more easily with and around a Sagittarius than with any other sign. If it is your good fortune to be in love with a Sagittarian or with someone who has a lot of Sagittarius in their natal charts, know that Valentine's Day is generally a cake walk. What they lack in stability, they make up for in lust for life and *joie de vivre*. And that is *soooooo* delightfully and deliciously contagious – being around a Sagittarius when they are in that mode is a gift in and of itself. For your Sagittarius, the Valentine's Day celebration you are creating needs to simply say, "*Let the games begin!*"

Excursions & Adventures: Take them to the racetrack, the polo club, or to New Orleans for Mardi Gras.

Valentine's Day Meal: Anything not from around here – definitely foreign food. The more exotic the better, preferably something like Moroccan, where you can sit on pillows on the floor, eat with your fingers, and watch the belly dancers.

Songs for the iPod: Reverend Horton Heat, "*Martini Time*"
The Cars, "*Let the Good Times Roll*"
The Band, "*Downtown in New Orleans*"
Bruce Springsteen, "*Thunder Road*"
Billy Joel, "*Only the Good Die Young*"
Little Feat, "*Let it Roll Tonite*"

Books for the Library: A Thomas Brother's Guide

DVD: "*Around the World in 80 Days*"
"*Under the Tuscan Sun*"
"*The Wedding Crashers*"
"*The Twilight Zone*" box set

Tickets to something: Plane tickets to a dude ranch in Wyoming or a resort at some tropical paradise.

Clothing: A bib and a crash helmet; one of those beer drinking hats that holds two cans and a straw; a riding habit, complete with boots, jodhpurs, and a crop; Levi's 501 boot cut jeans and cowboy boots.

Foreplay: A night on the town with the 3 D's (dining, drinking and dancing).

Mantra to help you get on the right page:
Carpe Diem (Seize the Day).

December 21 – January 20

Capricorn

Capricorn

Unlike Sagittarius, Capricorn is nothing but stable, reliable, predictable, and dependable. Ruled by Saturn, the lord of traditions and legacies, obligations and responsibilities, Capricorn doesn't like or appreciate fads, trends, or risk-taking. Nor does it like to waste time on flirtations and flings. Both personally and profession-ally, Capricorn is all business. They don't need love as much as they need to know they are safe. They need security, lots and lots of security. Given that, if your lover is a Capricorn or has a lot of Capricorn in their natal charts, your path to Valentine's Day bliss is very simple and very, very clear. Don't dally or rely on the subtly understated. Don't just get flowers, get a dozen red roses. The chocolates don't have to come in a heart shaped box, but they do have to be the very best, high quality chocolates. And if you can get it wholesale, you will have earned their respect. Your Valentine's Day gift needs to say, *"I am worthy of you and the investment you have made in me (and I pay very handsome dividends …)."*

Excursions & Adventures: Fort Knox; Wall Street; a personal audience with either the Federal Reserve Chair or Warren Buffet, preferably both; Switzerland.

Valentine's Day Meal: Either the most expensive place in town or someplace where you got a great deal.

Songs for the iPod: The Boston Pops, *"1812 Overture"*
Doris Day, *"Que Sera, Sera"*
Pink Floyd, *"Money"*
Simon & Garfunkel, *"I Am a Rock"*
Joel Grey, *"Money Makes the World Go Around"*

Books for the Library: *"Smart Couples Finish Rich"*
A subscription to *"Forbes Magazine"*
Anything by Suze Orman or about economics.
The biographies of Adam Smith and Andrew Carnegie.

DVD: Anything in black and white, preferably before the talkies. Anything from the History Channel.

Trinket: A watch, a calendar, or chewable calcium supplements.

Tickets to something: No tickets. Cash.

Clothing: Enduring, classic pieces in either neutral or versatile colors, expensive and well made: a little black dress for her, a London Fog raincoat for him.

Foreplay: Balance the checkbook, research stocks, indexes, and mutual funds, or play "I'll show you mine if you'll show me yours" with your Dun & Bradstreet ratings.

Mantra to help you get on the right page:
As you wish, sir/madam.

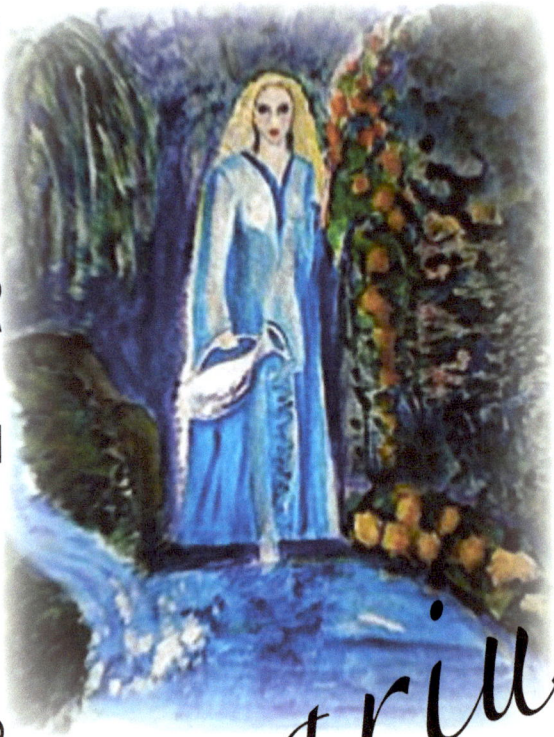

JANUARY 21 - FEBRUARY 20

Aquarius

Aquarius

In stark, glaring contrast to Capricorn, Aquarians are the most eccentric and unusual lovers. With one, you'll exist in a near permanent state of post-traumatic stress syndrome because you never know what's coming next, but by the same token, you will never, ever, ever be bored. You can count on them to be predictably unpredictable. The only tricky part is finding the fine line between the wildly exciting and the utterly and demoralizingly chaotic. If your lover is an Aquarian, or has a lot of Aquarius in their natal chart, you will definitely need to be thinking outside the box. In fact, don't go near the box. Don't even look at the box. Aquarius rules the unconventional and nontraditional, and to be successful with one of this sign you are just going to have to get with the program. You will also need a couple of contingency plans, for your Aquarian lover is highly likely to surprise you with a few plans of their own, none of which you could have foreseen. Regardless of what you buy or do, your Valentine's Day experience needs to say, "*Your surprises delight me.*"

Excursions & Adventures: Put them in the car and take them somewhere, but don't tell them where you are going. Blindfold them if necessary.

Valentine's Day Meal: Space Food Sticks, Tang, and T.V. dinners while watching Shuttle launches and landings, "*The Universe,*" or any of the Science Channel's programming on your brand new plasma flat screen.

Songs for the iPod: Anything by The Clash.
David Bowie, "*Space Oddity*"
Lou Reed, "*Walk on the Wild Side*"
Lipps, Inc., "*Funky Town*"

Books for the Library: "*String Theory for Dummies*"
Anything by Stephen Hawking.

DVD: "*2001: A Space Odyssey*"
"*The Rocky Horror Picture Show*"
Anything Gene Roddenberry had anything to do with.

Trinket: No Trinkets. Electronic gadgets from Radio Shack.

Tickets to something: The Home Electronics Expo in Vegas; any of the annual Future Expos. Though you will get bonus points for the Nano Technology one in Milan.

Clothing: Doesn't matter much, as long as it is made of non-natural, 100% man-made materials.

Wild Card: A divining rod.

Mantra to help you get on the right page:
… to boldly go where no man has gone before …

FEBRUARY 21 - MARCH 20

Pisces

Pisces

Piscean lovers can be the most difficult to handle of all the signs of the zodiac. Ever try to hold a fish? Those babies can really move, even when they are not scared and/or not out of their element. On land or sea, you can count on your Pisces to pretty much always be moving back and forth between desperately needing a container and actively rebelling against it. But take heart, while it may be some hard work, *nobody* - and I mean **nobody** - loves you as completely as a Pisces. I mean down to your soul's core. Past that, down to the very fiber of your being, to the cellular level. Down to your DNA. Seriously. If your beloved is a Pisces or has a lot of Pisces in their natal chart, your Valentine's gift needs to say a couple of things. First and foremost it needs to say *"I have you and you are free."* I know. It may sound fishy to you, but your Piscean will both understand it and love you for it.

Excursions & Adventures: A whale watching trip; a cruise in a glass-bottomed boat. Snorkeling, scuba diving, or surfing.

Valentine's Day Meal: Seafood, preferably someplace on or within sight of the water.

Songs for the iPod: Pink Floyd, *"Comfortably Numb"*
Black Flag, *"TV Party Tonite"*
Green Day, *"Wake Me Up When September Ends"*
The song Gollum sings to his fish in *"The Two Towers"*

Books for the Library: Masaru Emoto, *"The Secret Life of Water"*
"One Fish, Two Fish, Red Fish, Blue Fish"

DVD: *"The Poseidon Adventure"*
"Finding Nemo"
"The Days of Wine and Roses"
"The Lost Weekend"
"Resurrection"

Trinket: An aquarium, with fish.

Tickets to something: The Seaquarium.

Clothing: Anything billowy, opalescent and diaphanous. Anything that has several layers to it or makes you look and feel like Isadora Duncan.

Wild Card: A swimming pool.

Mantra to help you get on the right page:
Anchor this boat, lest it become a ship of fools.

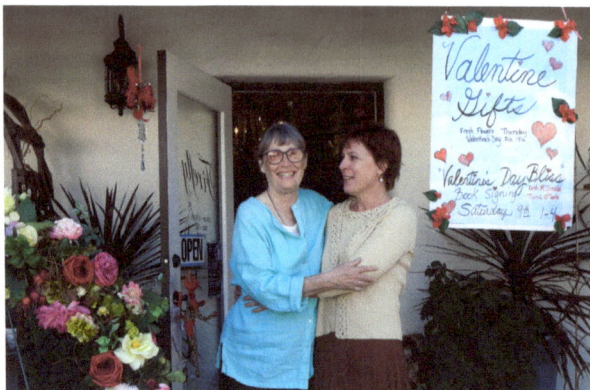

From left,, Jamie O'Toole and Beth McDonald at a book signing in 2008.
(photo by Kim Fisher)

About the Authors

Jamie O'Toole began her study of astrology via a series of happy accidents while she was living in Europe in 1964. First Jamie discovered a copy of Lady Ingrid Lynde Frasier's "Astrology and Common Sense" while she was in Greece. She thoroughly enjoyed the tome, and it began to change the way she thought and the way she was present in her life. Shortly thereafter, while in London, Jamie's car broke down. While it was being repaired, Jamie realized that Lady Frasier lived right around the corner. Jamie called her and was fortunate enough to not only meet with her, but to begin studying with her. Thus began a lifelong journey.

Beth McDonald's study of astrology began rather similarly about 30 years later. Already a practicing psychic, Beth was invited to one of Jennifer Freed's astrology classes, the precursor to her current ACS program. She was hooked from the first minute of the first class. Beth continued to study and learn, and when she became confident of her proficiency, Beth began to incorporate astrology into her readings.

Jamie and Beth met (in this lifetime) in 1996 or 1997, when Jamie heard one of Beth's ads on KZBN radio and called her. They have been friends from that moment on, and the rest is history. Together, Beth and Jamie have spent countless hours studying the many different astrological theories and theorists. They have analyzed countless astrology charts for a vast array of people and groups, from a variety of different angles and for amazingly interesting reasons. The trends and tendencies revealed by those experiences led them to start writing books and articles. Both Jamie and Beth live in Santa Barbara with their respective families.

.

www.ingramcontent.com/pod-product-compliance
Lightning Source LLC
Chambersburg PA
CBHW041224270326
41933CB00001B/38